The shuttle is 37 metres long, with a wingspan of 25 metres. It can carry 29,500 kg of cargo. Here it is carrrying the European Space Agency's Spacelab and other experimental equipment.

Tail fin

Rudder

Engine pod

Heat-resistant tiles (below) protect the underside, wing edges and nose of the orbiter from temperatures of over 2,000°C during re-entry. Every tile is different, like a huge jigsaw puzzle.

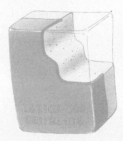

The main engines are used only during launch. Two orbital manoeuvring system (OMS) engines move the craft inito different orbits and slow it down for its return to Earth. Small changes in speed and position are made using 44 small thrusters. Rudder and 'elevons' control the orbiter's gliding descent. The rudder opens in two halves to slow the shuttle for landing.

Like an ordinary aircraft, the shuttle is built on a framework of lightweight aluminium-alloy spars, and has a retractable undercarriage. In orbit, the payload doors are opened; radiators on their insides help disperse the heat generated by all the electrical equipment on board.

Carbon-covered leading edge

Elevon

ADVENTURES IN THE REAL WORLD

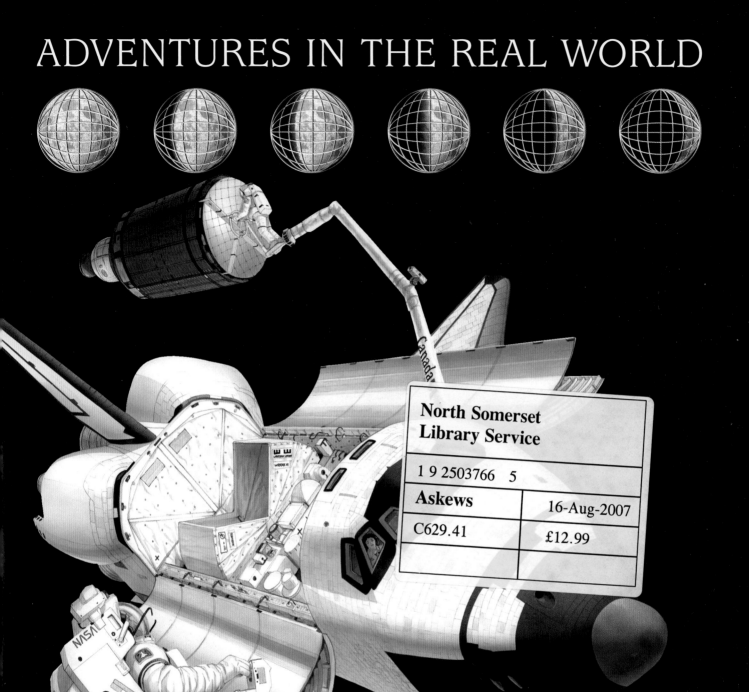

The story of the

Exploration of Space

BOOK HOUSE

1 3 5 7 9 8 6 4 2

Published in Great Britain in 2007 by
Book House, an imprint of
The Salariya Book Company Ltd
25 Marlborough Place, Brighton BN1 1UB
www.salariya.com
www.book-house.co.uk

HB ISBN-13: 978-1-905638-16-1
PB ISBN-13:.978-1-905638-17-8

SALARIYA

A CIP catalogue record for this book is available
from the British Library.

Printed and bound in China.
Printed on paper from sustainable sources.

Author: Penny Clarke
Illustrators: David Antram, Mark Bergin
and Bill Donohoe
Consultant: Dr. Luke Chatburn
Editor: Stephen Haynes
Editorial Assistant: Mark Williams

Penny Clarke is an author and editor specialising in
children's information books. She lives in Norfolk.

Dr Luke Chatburn is a specialist in Machine Vision.
He also works with the International Space School
Educational Trust, a non-profit company dedicated to
the promotion of space science in UK schools.

CONTENTS

DREAMS OF SPACE TRAVEL

Chinese rockets

Today space travel is a reality – for a few people. But did our distant ancestors dream about it too, as they gazed at the Moon and stars? It's impossible to know, but myths tell us they certainly dreamed of flying. That dream did not come true until the 20th century, although there had been many attempts before then. The Chinese invented rockets at least 800 years ago. Unfortunately rockets proved useful weapons, then as now. But one day it would be a rocket that helped humans into space.

THE MOON

Is it a man or is it a hare? Throughout history people have 'seen' shapes in the Moon's surface features.

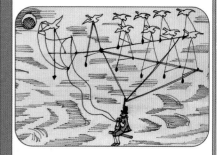

Space fantasy: in a 16th-century book, swans towed the hero to the Moon.

Space fiction: Jules Verne's 1865 novel *From the Earth to the Moon* influenced serious scientists.

THE FIRST ROCKETS – INVENTED IN CHINA ABOUT 800 YEARS AGO

The Chinese, who had invented gunpowder centuries earlier, were making rockets as weapons by 1232, if not before. They used bamboo tubes packed with explosives.

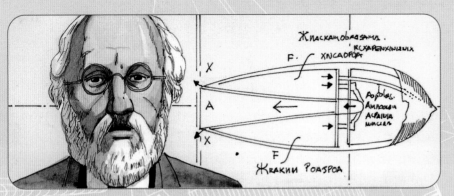

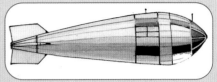

Tsiolkovsky was right: multistage rockets do overcome gravity.

The Russian scientist Konstantin Tsiolkovsky (1857–1935) is known as the father of space travel. He did pioneering work on multistage rockets, believing only they could overcome Earth's gravity. In 1903 he suggested that liquid fuel would be best for powering rockets.

Goddard's first rocket, fuelled by petrol and liquid oxygen, rose 12 metres in the air before falling back to the ground.

Like Tsiolkovsky, the American scientist Robert H. Goddard (1882–1945) realised it was rockets powered by liquid fuel that would make space travel a reality. In 1929 he built the first high-altitude rocket.

During World War II, German scientist Wernher von Braun developed the V-2 rocket. Packed with explosives and powered by liquid fuel, over 1400 of them were fired at London.

AMAZING FACT

On 16 March 1926 Goddard successfully launched the first liquid-fuelled rocket at Auburn, Massachusetts, USA. This is considered by flight historians to be as significant as the Wright Brothers' flight at Kitty Hawk.

THE FIRST SPACE TRAVELLERS

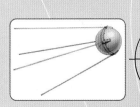

Sputnik 1, the first man-made satellite

Soon after World War II ended in 1945, another war began. It is known as the Cold War, and was fought by the US and the Soviet Union (now Russia). The fighting was not between armed forces out in the open, but by scientists in secret laboratories. It was really a political war, although the technologies the scientists developed could have produced weapons more powerful and more destructive than anything yet seen. The Americans, certain they had the best scientists and facilities, were horrified when on 4 October 1957, the Soviet Union sent the satellite *Sputnik 1* into space.

SPUTNIK 1

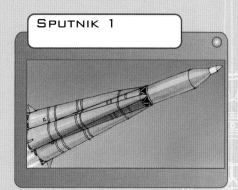

An SS-6 rocket put *Sputnik 1* into orbit. Soviet scientists had proved Tsiolkovsky and Goddard right: rockets could escape Earth's gravity.

SPUTNIK 2

The next month, November 1957, the Soviet Union sent the first living creature – a dog called Laika – into space in the larger *Sputnik 2*.

A NEW RECRUIT

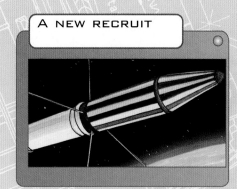

US efforts to build rockets were unsuccessful at first: at least one exploded on the launch pad. In desperation they recruited Wernher von Braun, now a US citizen, to design their rockets.

FIRST LIVING THING IN SPACE: LAIKA THE DOG

Sadly, Laika did not survive her space trip. The heat in the capsule was too great, and she died within hours of going into orbit.

SOVIET COSMONAUT IN TEST FLIGHT

YURI GAGARIN: FIRST MAN IN SPACE

The Soviet Union's successful space programme continued as they developed larger satellites and more powerful rockets. Then, on 12 April 1961, after more test flights using animals, they launched the first human into space. Yuri Gagarin, a Soviet cosmonaut (the English word is 'astronaut'), made one orbit around the Earth before returning safely.

The rocket taking Gagarin into space blasts off.

Gagarin's spacecraft *Vostok 1* (Russian for 'East') was 4.8 metres long, but the capsule was only 2.3 metres in diameter.

THE VIEW FROM SPACE

As *Vostok 1* carried him up through the Earth's atmosphere, Gagarin had views of Earth that no-one else had ever seen.

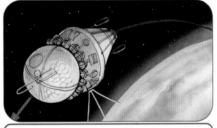

ORBITING THE EARTH

Vostok 1 travelled at more than 27,000 km/h as it made its single orbit around the Earth. Then it slowed in preparation for re-entry.

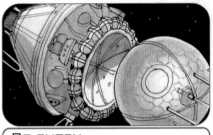

RE-ENTRY

After take-off, re-entry is the riskiest manoeuvre. Get the speed and angle wrong, and the spacecraft burns up.

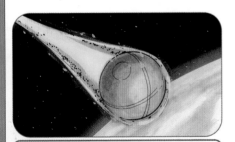

FIREBALL!

As it re-entered the Earth's atmosphere the capsule looked like a fireball. Inside, Gagarin felt the strong G-forces as the capsule slowed down.

LEAVING THE CAPSULE

Re-entry was perfect. Then Gagarin ejected at 7,000 metres. (The Soviets denied this at first, perhaps to make their achievement seem greater.)

BACK TO EARTH

Gagarin parachuted gently back to Earth, landing near the River Volga in Russia. Parachutes also brought the capsule down safely. A very successful space mission!

THE SPACE RACE STARTS

A Mercury space capsule, used for American space missions 1961–3

The Soviet Union's success was a huge embarrassment to the US, which in 1958 had formed the National Aeronautics and Space Administration (NASA) specifically to put a man in space. By early 1961 NASA had sent a chimpanzee on a short space flight, but work was still needed on the rockets. Then came news of Gagarin's flight. Stung by this, the new US president, John F. Kennedy, pledged in May 1961 that the US would put a man on the Moon and bring him back safely by 1970. This was a challenge to the Soviet Union – the *Space Race* was on.

After his pledge, President Kennedy ensured NASA had ample funds for the space programme.

In 1962, US astronaut John Glenn orbited the Earth three times. His spacecraft landed in the Atlantic Ocean.

15 MINUTES OF ORBITAL FLIGHT BY ALAN SHEPARD

Alan Shepard's 5 May 1961 launch in *Freedom 7* was a key turning point in the Space Race. He was the first American astronaut in space, and although Gagarin had got there a few weeks earlier, the US was now starting to catch up.

The US satellite *Telstar* was launched in 1962.

MERCURY - NASA'S FIRST
MANNED SPACE VEHICLES

Although these successes
boosted NASA, they were still
behind. In 1965, cosmonaut
Alexei Leonov made the first
space 'walk'. Later that year,
America's Edward White also
walked in space.

*The Mercury capsules (above), used
between 1961 and 1963, were the first
US spacecraft.*

Another 'first' for the Soviet Union was in 1963,
when Valentina Tereshkova became the first
woman in space. She orbited Earth 48 times in
three days.

Launched in 1964, *Voskhod* ('Sunrise') *1* was the
first spacecraft to have an air-filled cabin, so the
cosmonauts on board did not need spacesuits.

EARLY SOVIET SPACECRAFT

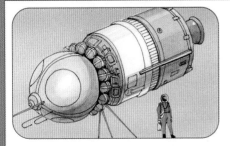

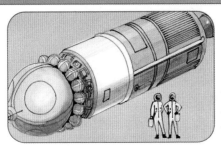

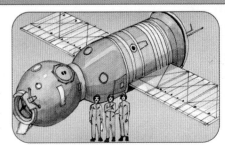

Vostok was the first of the three
different spacecraft developed
for the Soviet Union's space
programme in the 1960s.

As space flights became longer,
spacecraft needed larger crews.
By 1964 Soviet engineers had
adapted *Vostok* to make the
three-person *Voskhod*.

Then, in 1967, *Soyuz* ('Union')
was launched. Sadly, its first
mission was a disaster – it
crashed after making 18 orbits.

PREPARING FOR APOLLO

Gemini capsule, 1965

By the mid-1960s NASA scientists were under pressure: there was still a lot of work to do before landing a man on the Moon, let alone by 1970. They had some successes. After Alexei Leonov's spacewalk, he had great difficulty getting back through the hatch into the spacecraft, but Edward White did not have this problem. And Leonov's spacecraft missed its landing site by 3,200 kilometres.

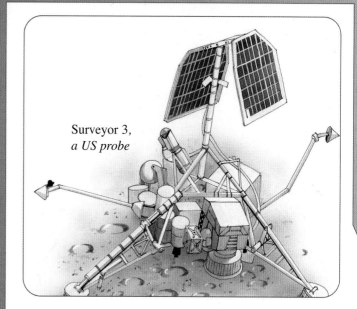

Surveyor 3, *a US probe*

As the technology for putting a man on the Moon improved, attention turned to the Moon itself. Would it be suitable for a landing? Would a spacecraft crash into a crater, or sink into the thick dust? Both the US and the Soviet Union sent unmanned craft, called probes, to find out.

FIRST AMERICAN ASTRONAUT TO SPACEWALK: EDWARD WHITE, JUNE 1965

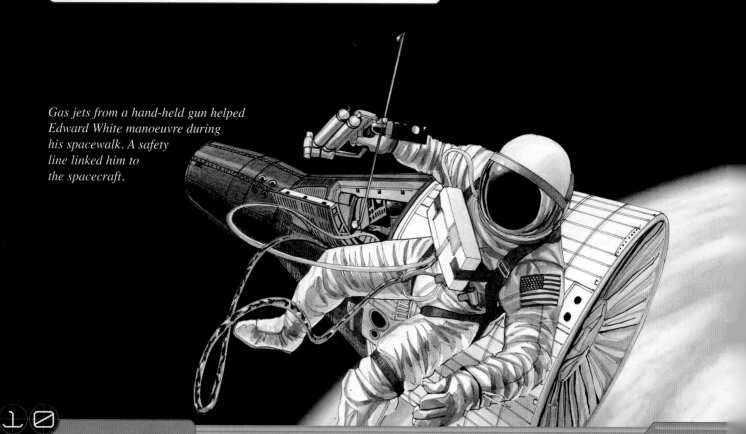

Gas jets from a hand-held gun helped Edward White manoeuvre during his spacewalk. A safety line linked him to the spacecraft.

Fuel, oxidant and pressure tanks

Retro-rocket

In 1965 NASA introduced the Gemini 3 spacecraft, with a crew of two, to replace the Mercury capsules. Astronauts in Gemini controlled the craft and practised manoeuvring in space. One of the most important manoeuvres was docking (joining) with another craft, as you would need to do this to get back from the Moon.

Command pilot

Landing parachute storage

Attitude control thruster

Pilot and extra-vehicular activity (spacewalk) astronaut

Instrument panel

Re-entry attitude thruster

Rendezvous radar

This was because the Apollo spacecraft that went to the Moon would have two parts: command module and Moon lander. At the Moon they would separate, with the lander descending to the Moon and later rejoining the command ship to return to Earth.

AMAZING FACTS

In Greek mythology, Apollo was the god who guided travellers on their way.

In the mid-1960s NASA's Jet Propulsion Laboratory developed digital image processing to allow computer enhancement of Moon pictures. Similar technology is now used by doctors and hospitals to look at images of organs inside the human body.

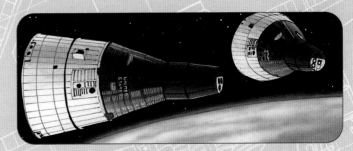

During the planned Moon mission, two Apollo craft would have to dock (join together) in space. Getting this right was absolutely vital. Between 1965 and 1969 astronauts practised this manoeuvre in the Gemini craft. In 1965 Gemini 5 and Gemini 6 approached within a few metres of each other.

APOLLO 1 AND APOLLO 8

Dark areas on the moon are known as 'seas', although we know there is no water there

The first Apollo spacecraft left Earth in 1968. The US space programme had suffered several setbacks, including the *Apollo 1* disaster (right). And there were so many unknowns. What was on the far side of the Moon? Would the spacecraft burn up on re-entering the Earth's atmosphere? What about the effects of weightlessness? Computer modelling gave some clues, but only a manned mission would provide firm answers. In December 1968, *Apollo 8* lifted off to do just that.

In 1967 the Apollo space programme had a major disaster. The three-man crew of *Apollo 1* died when fire destroyed the spacecraft on its launch pad. As a result, less flammable materials were used for later craft.

PRACTICE MAKES PERFECT: USING TOOLS AND BULKY SPACE SUITS ON A MOCK-UP OF THE LUNAR SURFACE

Astronauts had intensive training. On a mock-up of the Moon's surface, they learnt to move around and use tools while wearing bulky spacesuits. The mission controllers kept the trainee astronauts on their toes by surprising them with all sorts of emergencies to see how they dealt with them.

Weightlessness was simulated in a training aeroplane. So many people got airsick in this plane that it was nicknamed the 'Vomit Comet'.

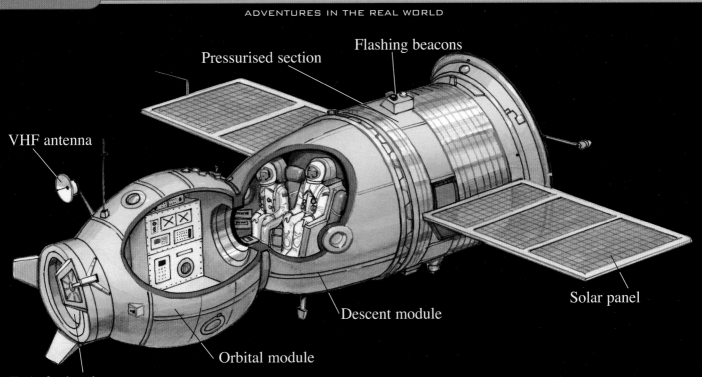

Pressurised section

Flashing beacons

VHF antenna

Solar panel

Descent module

Orbital module

Transfer hatch

Meanwhile, the Russians were also trying to send men to the Moon. The USSR launched its first Soyuz spacecraft in 1967. It could carry crews of two or three cosmonauts. Russians still use Soyuz vehicles to this day.

APOLLO 8 MISSION

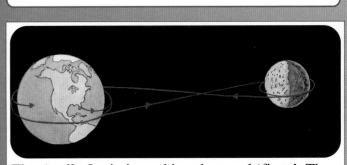

The *Apollo 8* mission achieved several 'firsts'. The three astronauts were the first to leave the Earth's orbit. And, on 24 December 1968, they were the first to see the far side of the Moon.

Apollo 8 orbited the Moon for 20 hours before returning safely. There was anxiety when NASA lost contact with it on the far side of the Moon, which blocked the radio signals. The crew saw huge craters pitting the Moon's surface, caused by meteors crashing onto it.

THE SATURN V ROCKET

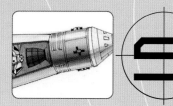

Detail of Saturn V

Spacecraft need very powerful forces to get them beyond the pull of Earth's gravity, and Wernher von Braun's Saturn rockets provided that force. The first six Apollo missions were designed specifically to test the Saturn rocket. The success of *Apollo 8* took the programme to its next stage: landing astronauts on the Moon.

The crew of *Apollo 9* practised docking the command ship and lunar module while still in Earth's orbit.

In May 1969 *Apollo 10* took off to test the lunar module. A Moon landing could only go ahead if this mission was completely successful – too much was at stake to risk failure.

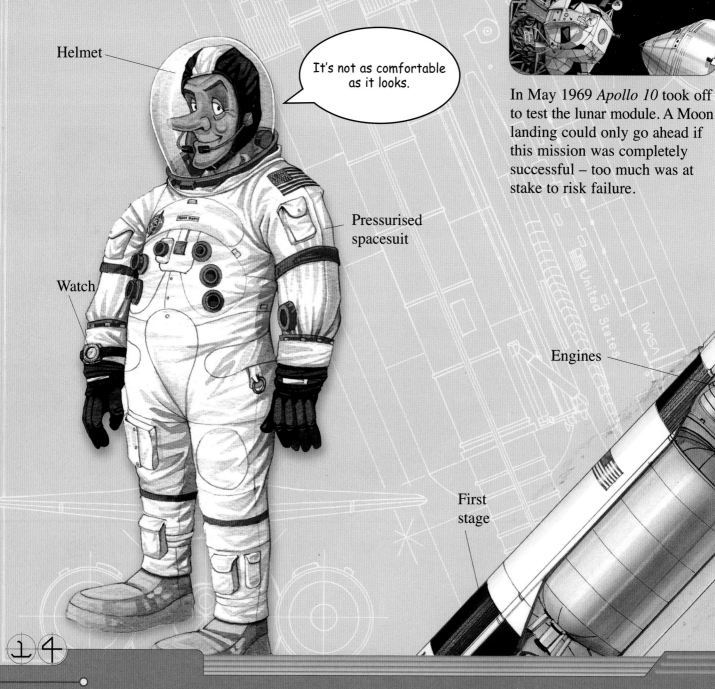

Helmet

It's not as comfortable as it looks.

Pressurised spacesuit

Watch

Engines

First stage

Launch escape system

Command module (*Columbia*)

Service module

Lunar module (*Eagle*)

The Saturn V was the largest rocket ever built – it had to be, because *Apollo 11* was too heavy for any of von Braun's earlier rockets. The rocket had three parts (stages) and was designed just to get *Apollo 11* beyond the pull of Earth's gravity. As each stage used up its fuel it was jettisoned (cast off).

Third stage

Second stage

AMAZING FACT

Saturn V was huge: 111 metres tall. The building at Cape Canaveral, Florida, in which it was assembled is so tall that clouds sometimes gather around its top! The rocket's fuel was a mixture of liquid oxygen and kerosene. At take-off it used 15 tonnes per second.

During the *Apollo 10* mission two of the astronauts took the lunar module down to 14,460 metres above the Moon's surface. Then they fired its rockets to return to the command module.

To the horror of NASA's scientists, just three days before the launch of *Apollo 11*, the Soviet Union sent the unmanned spacecraft *Luna 15* to the Moon. But *Luna 15* crashed on the Moon and was destroyed.

APOLLO 11 LIFTS OFF

Ready to go!

Apollo 11's launch was scheduled for 16 July 1969. The three astronauts were flight commander Neil Armstrong, Michael Collins, pilot of the command module, and Buzz Aldrin, who would descend to the Moon with Armstrong in the lunar module. Two hours before take-off the astronauts took their seats in the command module and the entry hatch was closed. At last the waiting was over as Mission Control said 'You are go for launch'.

Mission Control in Houston, Texas was the command centre for Apollo's flight.

Early on 16 July the astronauts enjoyed breakfast. Then they put on their spacesuits and were taken to the launch pad, where preparations for take-off were underway.

BLAST-OFF!

Mission badge

As *Saturn V*'s engines lifted the huge rocket into the air they made one of the loudest noises ever heard.

1 Lift-off

7 Splashdown

Earth

2 *Columbia* docks with *Eagle*

THE LAUNCH

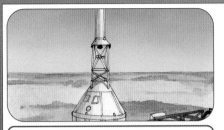

READY FOR LAUNCH

Saturn V was so huge that filling its fuel tanks took over five hours. It carried 2,000 tonnes of highly explosive fuel.

IGNITION!

When the engines ignited, a ball of flame appeared at the end of the rocket and the ground shook as it blasted off.

THREE-STAGE ROCKET

By making Saturn V in three sections it could be made lighter. This also had the advantage of reducing the fuel it used.

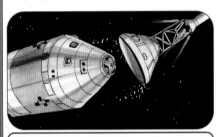

ESCAPE TOWER JETTISONED

Three minutes after take-off the launch escape tower, which had been fitted over the command module, was jettisoned.

IGNITION OF THIRD STAGE

Nine minutes after take-off Saturn's second stage had used its fuel and was jettisoned, leaving the third stage to continue alone.

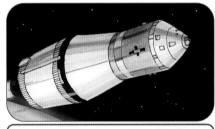

INTO ORBIT

Eleven minutes after take-off, *Apollo 11* and the third stage of Saturn reached the Earth's orbit. Next destination: the Moon!

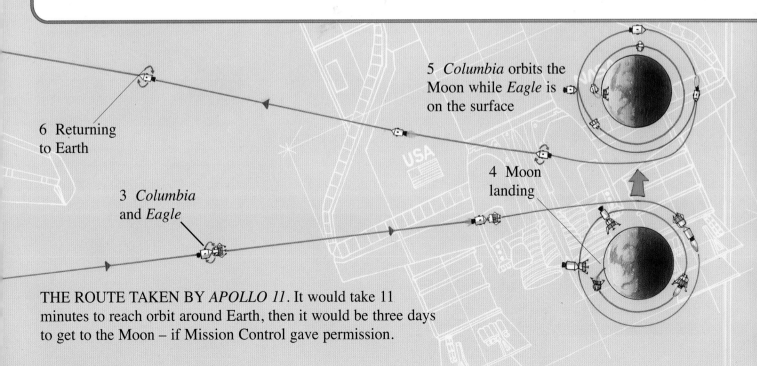

6 Returning to Earth

5 *Columbia* orbits the Moon while *Eagle* is on the surface

3 *Columbia* and *Eagle*

4 Moon landing

THE ROUTE TAKEN BY *APOLLO 11*. It would take 11 minutes to reach orbit around Earth, then it would be three days to get to the Moon – if Mission Control gave permission.

COLUMBIA AND EAGLE

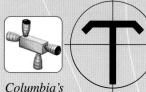

Columbia's thrusters

Three hours after *Apollo 11*'s launch, Mission Control told the astronauts they could head for the Moon. Once they were beyond the Earth's orbit, Michael Collins had to make a vital manoeuvre. *Eagle*, the lunar module, was inside the third stage. He had to detach *Columbia* and the service module from the rocket, turn them around, return to the rocket, and dock with *Eagle*.

COLLINS MANOEUVRES COMMAND MODULE TOWARDS *EAGLE*

I steer the spacecraft using hand controllers to fire rocket thrusters on the service module.

As *Columbia* approached Saturn V's third stage, panels protecting *Eagle* were jettisoned. The lunar module was too fragile to fly in Earth's atmosphere. Small rocket thrusters on each side of the service module helped Collins manoeuvre towards *Eagle*.

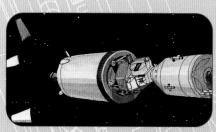

Columbia and *Eagle* docked successfully. Then Collins reversed *Columbia* to disengage *Eagle* from the third stage of Saturn V. Now, with *Eagle* firmly in place on the front of *Columbia*, the astronauts headed to the Moon, leaving the third stage of Saturn V behind.

Tracking light

Broad feet
to spread
the weight

Eagle *had only
one rocket to take
it back to
Columbia.*

Docking was vital
for Apollo's success.
If *Eagle* could not be
retrieved from Saturn V,
the Moon landing would be
impossible. If docking failed
when *Eagle* returned from the
Moon's surface, at least two
astronauts would die.

Landing gear

Lunar surface
sensing probe

NASA

COMMAND MODULE

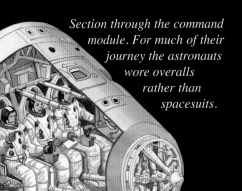

*Section through the command
module. For much of their
journey the astronauts
wore overalls
rather than
spacesuits.*

USA

The first docking was successful
and *Eagle* descended to the
Moon. Fuel was getting low
when Armstrong realised it was
heading for a crater full of
rocks. If *Eagle* overturned,
he and Aldrin would be killed.

'ONE GIANT LEAP'

As the Moon has no rain or wind, the astronauts' footsteps will remain there for thousands of years

Mission Control was tense. Then: 'Houston, Tranquillity Base here. The *Eagle* has landed.' So US astronauts were first on the Moon. But the landing had almost failed – *Eagle* only had 20 seconds' worth of fuel left when it touched down. About six hours later Armstrong and Aldrin opened the hatch. As Armstrong stepped onto the Moon he said the now famous words: 'That's one small step for man, one giant leap for mankind.'

In the dangerous moments before landing, Aldrin had to tell Armstrong *Eagle*'s height and speed.

ONE SMALL STEP FOR MAN,
ONE GIANT LEAP FOR MANKIND

The Moon's surface has gravity only one-sixth as strong as the Earth's. The astronauts had trained for this, but moving around was awkward at first.

Hey, you should see this!

MEDALS AND MEMORIALS

Like most explorers who achieve a 'first', the astronauts planted their country's flag on the Moon. Because there is no wind, a metal rod holds it out. They left medals and badges (above left)

in memory of those who had died trying to make space travel possible, and a plaque (above) to mark the landing. On it are the words: 'We came in peace for all mankind.'

In their two-and-a-half hours on the Moon, the astronauts collected 22 kilos of rock and soil. Later analysis showed the rocks were like Earth's, but much older.

US flag

Laser-beam reflector for measuring distance precisely

TV camera

Antenna

Solar power cell

Sensors

UNITED STATES

Soil scoop

Seismometer

RETURN TO EARTH

Armstrong was the last to leave

After doing more experiments, setting up instruments to record 'Moonquakes' and a laser mirror to measure the exact distance between the Moon and the Earth, it was time to return to *Columbia*. Armstrong closed *Eagle*'s hatch and Aldrin fired the ascent engine. This was a nervous moment: every other system in the entire mission had a back-up, except this one. But all was well: the engine fired perfectly and *Eagle* rose for its rendezvous with *Columbia* and the return journey to Earth.

Astronauts added water to bags of freeze-dried food, such as chicken and rice, before squeezing the 'meal' into their mouth.

INSTANT FOOD IN PLASTIC BAGS

Just like mother used to make...

TAKE-OFF FROM THE MOON

Eagle's ascent from the Moon went smoothly. It, too, left a memento of the landing: the framework which had supported it on the Moon's surface.

THE LONELY ASTRONAUT

In *Columbia*, on the far side of the Moon, Michael Collins had no contact with Earth or *Eagle*.

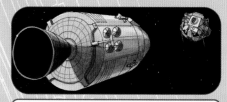

REUNITED

The astronauts must have been relieved to see the other craft. Docking was successful and the crew were reunited.

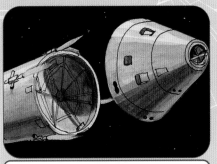

BACK TO EARTH

Columbia headed for Earth at 27,000 km/h, leaving *Eagle* behind. *Columbia* also separated from the service module, which was no longer needed.

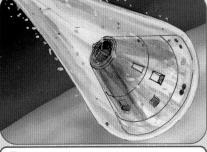

RE-ENTERING THE ATMOSPHERE

The intense heat generated by re-entering the Earth's atmosphere was a major danger. *Columbia*'s special covering fortunately withstood it.

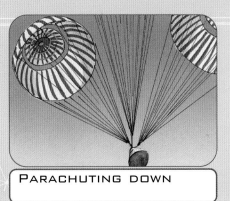

PARACHUTING DOWN

As *Columbia* descended towards Earth, huge parachutes stored in the nose-cone were released. These opened to slow the spacecraft down.

SPLASHING INTO THE PACIFIC

Columbia splashed down in the Pacific Ocean and immediately turned upside down. Balloons which had been stored in the nose-cone then inflated, turning it the right way up.

RESCUE!

A helicopter from USS *Hornet* arrived. The crew opened the hatch to greet the astronauts. The US really had sent men to the Moon and brought them back safely before 1970!

RETURN TO LAND

Winched into the helicopter, the astronauts were flown to *Hornet*. There they immediately went into a special isolation container, in case they had brought back deadly germs.

IN ISOLATION

As no human had been to the Moon before, no-one knew if the astronauts would return contaminated with germs against which humans had no natural protection. In addition, no one knew whether having been weightless would affect their health. President Nixon visited them in quarantine. But, after 20 days, doctors declared them healthy.

THE FINAL MOON MISSIONS

nother six Apollo Moon missions followed *Apollo 11*. Five were successful, but *Apollo 13* (right) almost ended in disaster. Meanwhile the Soviet Union, perhaps because it had lost the race to the Moon, concentrated on other aspects of space research, exploring space with unmanned probes. These were enormously expensive, but not as expensive as training cosmonauts. In addition, the Soviet Union put space stations into orbit around the Earth.

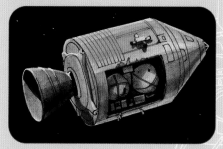

Two days after *Apollo 13*'s launch, an explosion damaged the command module's life-support system. Abandoning the Moon landing, the crew hoped the tiny lunar module would get them back safely. It did!

APOLLO 13 MISSION GOES BANG!

Houston, we have a problem...

AMAZING FACT

Before applying to become an astronaut, a pilot must have completed 1,000 hours of flying time in a jet aircraft.

In 1972 *Apollo 17* became the last manned Apollo mission to the Moon. Astronauts Eugene Cernan and Harrison Schmitt spent 22 hours there, exploring in a battery-powered lunar roving vehicle. It could travel up to six kilometres from the lunar module. The cost of Moon expeditions was enormous, but co-operation between countries would share costs.

Meteoroid showers were a natural danger. But a strong double outer layer protected spacecraft from the impact.

There were man-made dangers, too. With more and more space exploration, space 'litter' was becoming a problem. Colliding at speed with a dead satellite would be catastrophic.

LUNAR ROVING VEHICLE

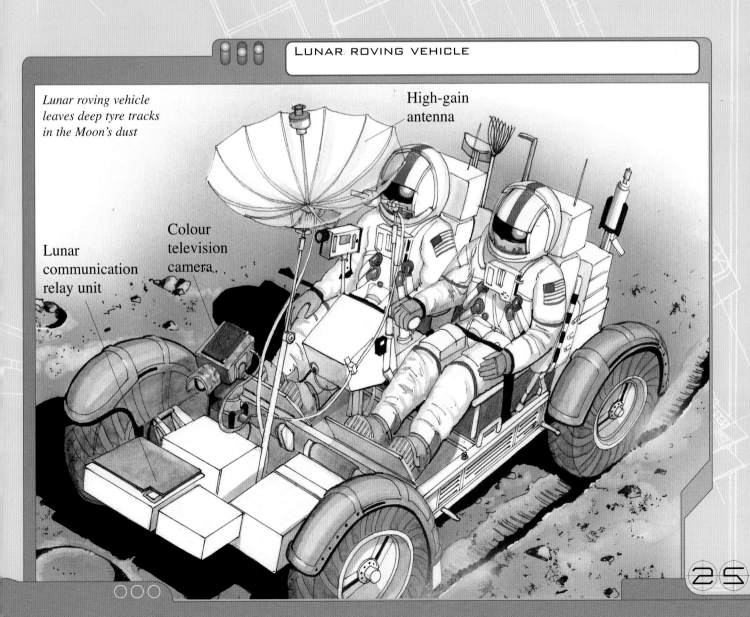

Lunar roving vehicle leaves deep tyre tracks in the Moon's dust

High-gain antenna

Colour television camera.

Lunar communication relay unit

SKYLAB AND SALYUT

The extreme weather conditions in space meant that the Skylab *crew had to rig up a sunshade to protect their ship*

The US had won the space race, but landing Armstrong and Aldrin on the Moon had cost NASA $22 billion. Although the Soviet Union did not release such information, western experts knew that their space programme cost much the same. In the US, interest in space exploration was fading: there were no obvious benefits, ordinary people were not involved, and it was wasteful – all those expensive machines were used only once.

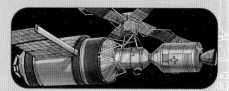

The Apollo lunar programme ended in December 1972. In May 1973 the US launched its first space station: *Skylab*. Mainly built from hardware developed for Apollo, it had a crew of three.

In 1974 cosmonauts spent a record 63 days in the Soviet Union's *Salyut* ('Salute') *4* space station. *Salyut 7*, the last of the series, was abandoned in 1986.

SOYUZ AND APOLLO MEET IN SPACE

They made it!

Meanwhile, down on Earth, there were congratulations all round – and possibly sighs of relief – at Mission Control.

In 1975 a Soviet Soyuz spacecraft docked with an American Apollo. The Soviet cosmonauts floated through the tunnel connecting the two craft to be greeted by the Americans. They were now colleagues, not competitors!

The Soviet Union's next space station was *Mir* ('Peace'). It was used from 20 February 1986 to March 2001, and crews spent up to six months at a time in it.

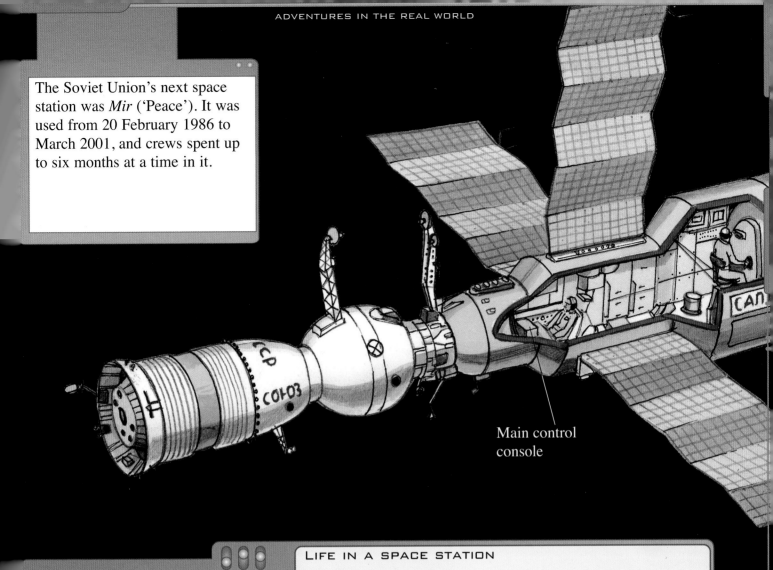

Main control console

LIFE IN A SPACE STATION

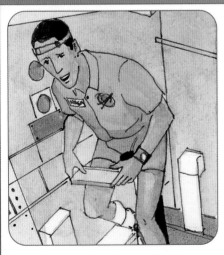

In microgravity, body fluids rise to the head, causing stick-thin legs and swollen faces. To overcome this, astronauts exercise hard every day.

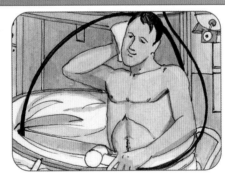

In the zero gravity of a spacecraft, water, like everything else, floats. This makes washing rather difficult! Spacecraft have specially designed showers so crews can keep clean.

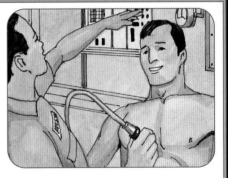

Astronauts have regular health checks to ensure they're fit. Humans have evolved to live in Earth's gravity, so keeping fit in conditions without gravity is essential. If people ever travel to other planets, they will have to spend very long periods weightless in space.

VOYAGERS IN THE SOLAR SYSTEM

The distances covered by spacecraft are vast. In 1977 NASA launched one of the most ambitious unmanned space probes while the planets Jupiter, Saturn, Uranus and Neptune would be in alignment – a very rare phenomenon. The plan was to launch two spacecraft, *Voyager 1* and *Voyager 2*, which would use the planets' gravity to send them even further into space. All went to plan and both Voyager spacecraft are still transmitting data as they head out of the solar system. In 2010 they will reach its very edge.

The Voyagers have made amazing discoveries as they make their 'Grand Tour' of the four planets. The Great Red Spot on Jupiter is actually a huge storm. Uranus has a previously unknown magnetic field and ten more moons than astronomers knew about. Triton, Neptune's largest moon, seems to have active geysers, but what is coming out of them? It will take years for scientists to analyse all the data, and more is still to come.

PATHS OF VOYAGERS 1 AND 2

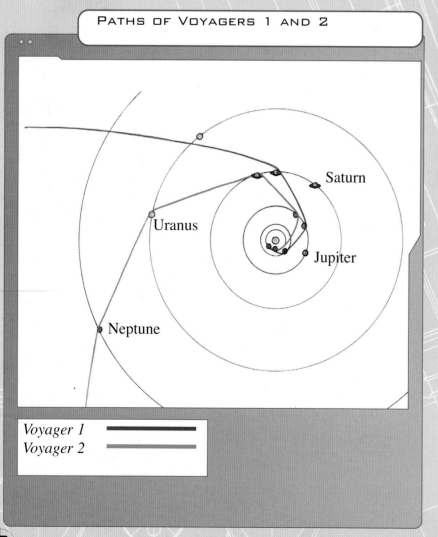

Saturn

Uranus

Jupiter

Neptune

Voyager 1 ━━━━━
Voyager 2 ━━━━━

AMAZING FACT

There are no sounds in space, because there is no air to carry sound waves.

Rings of Saturn

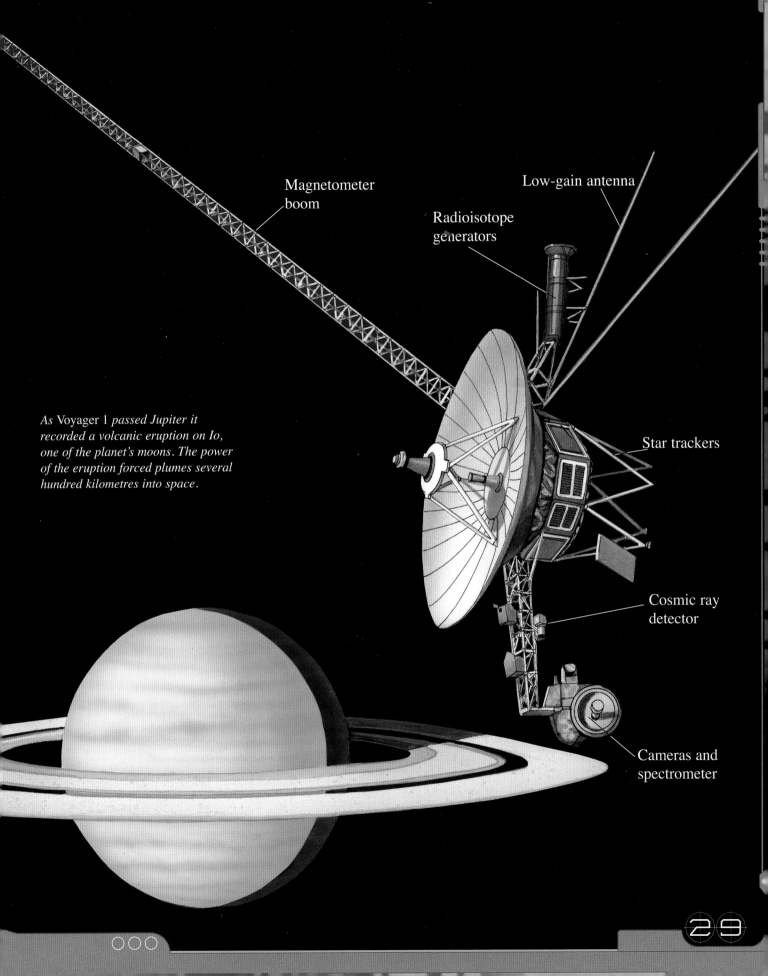

Magnetometer boom

Radioisotope generators

Low-gain antenna

Star trackers

Cosmic ray detector

Cameras and spectrometer

As Voyager 1 passed Jupiter it recorded a volcanic eruption on Io, one of the planet's moons. The power of the eruption forced plumes several hundred kilometres into space.

REUSABLE SPACECRAFT

X-15 rocket plane

Space exploration was expensive because it was so wasteful: the only part of a spacecraft reused was the crew! So, as public interest faded and NASA faced budget cuts, scientists sought ways to make it cheaper. Were reusable space vehicles a possibility? All spacecraft are subject to huge stresses and strains. For example, their speed causes tremendous heat and friction as they travel through space. So the safety challenge would be enormous.

M2F-1

X24B

X-15A-2

Three steps in designing a reusable spacecraft. The wingless M2F-1 and X24B were dropped onto a dried-up lake in test landings. The X-15A-2 rocket plane reached 7,311 km/h at altitudes of 98,816 metres.

WORLD'S FASTEST PLANE: X-15, MACH 6.7 (7,274 KM/H)

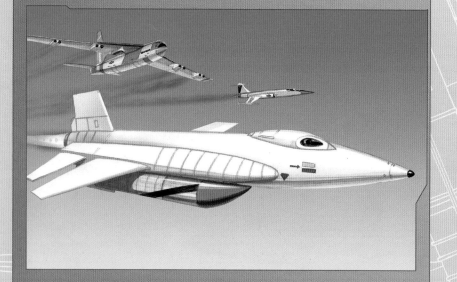

Would rocket planes be the answer? They were already being developed and Neil Armstrong had test-flown them.

AMAZING FACT

The X-15 aircraft made a total of 199 flights over a period of nearly 10 years from 1959 to 1968. It set new unofficial world speed and altitude records. Information gained from this highly successful programme contributed to the development of the Mercury, Gemini, and Apollo spacecraft and the Space Shuttle.

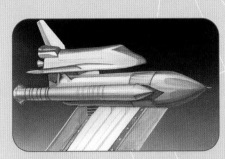

Gradually a practical craft began to take shape. The aerodynamics of take-off were tested on this model of a two-stage craft.

An adapted Boeing 747-100 carried a full-size dummy orbiter for landing tests (above). Orbiters would touch down on land, which was cheaper than landing at sea. Insulation was essential, otherwise the shuttle would burn up on re-entry. Reinforced carbon-carbon (RCC) covers the nose and the wings' leading edges, where the temperature reaches 1,650° C. Black high-temperature silica tiles cover the underneath and the tail's front edge. Elsewhere, white low-temperature tiles and insulation blankets are used.

Wind-tunnel tests were essential. A one-third scale model was used to test how it glided, and how air flowed around it when it re-entered Earth's gravity.

PREPARE FOR LIFT-OFF!

Astronauts training in deep-water tanks

Eventually it was clear that a two-stage space shuttle was best. The orbiter would be carried into space on a huge external fuel tank (ET) and two solid rocket boosters (SRBs), which it would leave behind. The orbiter, which has around 600,000 parts, is assembled and positioned on the ET in the Vehicle Assembly Building at the Kennedy Space Center, where the Saturn Vs were built in the 1960s – so this huge building too is being reused!

The giant crawler takes the shuttle to the launch site at a speed of 1.6 km/h.

ASTRONAUTS PRACTISE SPACEWALKS IN A HUGE WATER TANK

In at the deep end!

Astronauts train for weightlessness in large water tanks, like giant swimming pools, that NASA calls 'neutral buoyancy tanks'. Astronauts are weighed down so they neither float nor sink – simulating microgravity. Then they can practise important operations, such as repairing satellites.

Astronauts also train for weightlessness inside aircraft flying on a special curved path.

World's most powerful searchlights

The crawler is 40 metres long and 34.7 wide. Each link in its tracks is 2.3 metres long and weighs a tonne. For every 7 metres it travels, its two engines each use 4.5 litres of diesel. Besides the shuttle, ET and SRBs, the crawler carries the launch platform. It takes about six hours for a space shuttle on a crawler to make the trip from the Vehicle Assembly Building to the launch pad before a mission. A levelling system keeps the crawler level with the ground.

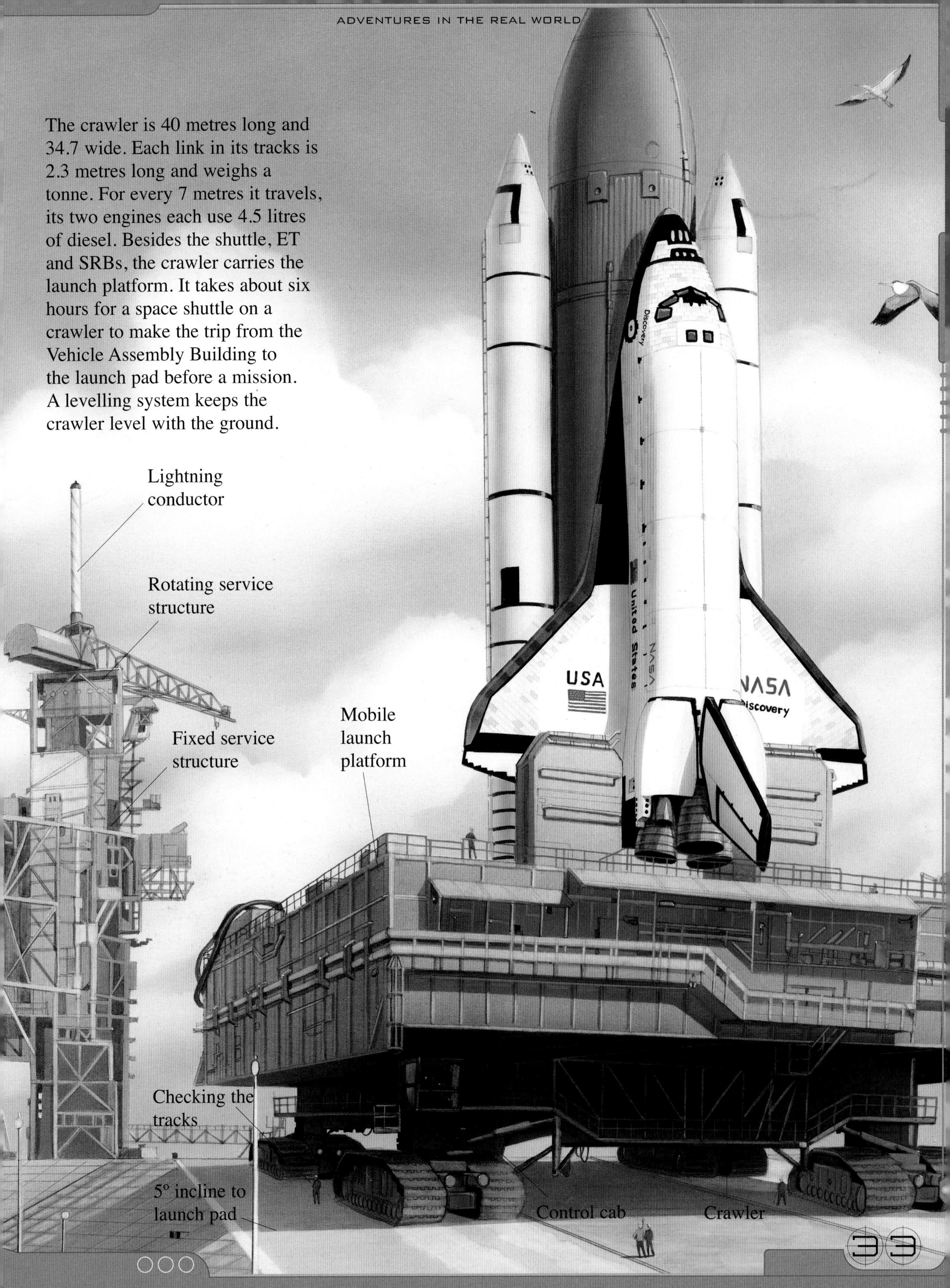

Lightning conductor
Rotating service structure
Fixed service structure
Mobile launch platform
USA
NASA
United States
Discovery
Checking the tracks
5º incline to launch pad
Control cab
Crawler

LIVING IN SPACE

The Remote Manipulator System (RMS) is essential for manoeuvring astronauts

Living in space has its problems, mostly due to reduced gravity. Unless fixed, everything floats – including the crew. Lack of gravity weakens the heart and other muscles, so astronauts use a treadmill every day. But they must be harnessed to it, otherwise they would float away. Astronauts keep themselves in place on the toilet with bendy bars. A vacuum flush sucks waste into a tank. The orbiter's air temperature and pressure are like Earth's, so astronauts wear T-shirts.

Microphone

Intercom connector

Sun visor

Attachments for parachute harness

J. BAGIAN

Large pockets

GETTING INTO A SPACESUIT

Astronauts have two spacesuits: a pressure suit (top right) for launch and re-entry, and the Extravehicular Mobility Unit (EMU) suit if they are going outside the shuttle. It has five layers:
1 Urine Containment System (UCS)
2 Liquid Cooling and Ventilation Garment (LCVG)
3 Lower Torso Assembly (LTA)
4 Hard Upper Torso (HUT)
5 Helmet.

1

2

3

NASA

NASA

3

4

5

SNEEZING

With your helmet on, how are you going to sneeze or scratch your nose?

ASTRONAUT IN A MANNED
MANOEUVRING UNIT (MMU)

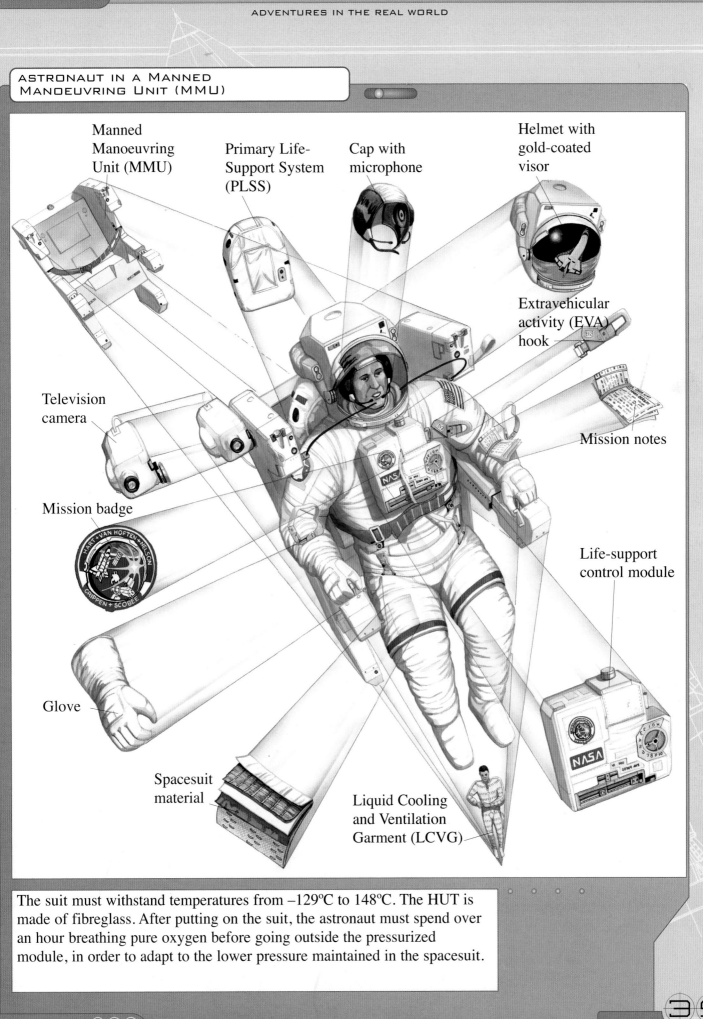

Manned
Manoeuvring
Unit (MMU)

Primary Life-
Support System
(PLSS)

Cap with
microphone

Helmet with
gold-coated
visor

Extravehicular
activity (EVA)
hook

Television
camera

Mission notes

Mission badge

HART • VAN HOFTEN • NELSON
GRIPPEN • SCOBEE

Life-support
control module

Glove

Spacesuit
material

Liquid Cooling
and Ventilation
Garment (LCVG)

The suit must withstand temperatures from –129°C to 148°C. The HUT is
made of fibreglass. After putting on the suit, the astronaut must spend over
an hour breathing pure oxygen before going outside the pressurized
module, in order to adapt to the lower pressure maintained in the spacesuit.

FROM LAUNCH TO RE-ENTRY

Thermal tile

The shuttle made its first flight in April 1981. At 6.6 seconds to lift-off, its three main engines ignited and the sound-suppression water system came on. This pumps over a million litres of water onto the launch pad to protect both it and the shuttle from the noise of the launch.

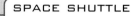

At launch, both main engines and SRBs steer the shuttle. When empty, the SRBs forced away by their nose rockets.

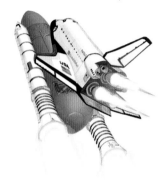

On re-entry, thermal tiles protect from enormous heat.

LIFT-OFF OF THE SPACE SHUTTLE

Two minutes after lift-off, the SRBs have used all their fuel. Small rockets at the front push them out, and away from the orbiter. They will parachute down into the sea, where they are then collected for reuse later.

Wheels are lowered at 532 metres above ground.

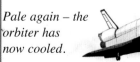

Pale again – the orbiter has now cooled.

The orbiter re-enters the Earth's atmosphere at 25 times the speed of sound. The autopilot then puts the orbiter into S-turns to reduce its speed. The first turn slows it by 5,630 km/h. Although the orbiter can land automatically, the mission commander usually takes control when the orbiter is 32 km from the runway.

The orbiter made its first landing on a dried-up lake at Edwards Air Force Base. Escorted by a T-38 training aircraft, and with service and safety crews on standby, it was a perfect landing. NASA was jubilant – they had shown it was possible to create a reusable spacecraft. Now space travel could be cheaper, and the shuttle could also be used to launch commercial payloads, such as communications satellites.

Eight minutes after launch, the empty ET is jettisoned.

EYE ON THE UNIVERSE

stronomers have a problem: they observe space through the Earth's atmosphere. Pollution makes the atmosphere dirty, so viewing distant objects is even more difficult. For years astronomers dreamt of overcoming this with a telescope in space. In April 1990 that dream came true when the Hubble Space Telescope (HST) was launched. At first there were problems with its main mirror – but the HST is designed to be serviced in space and the problems were overcome. Since then the images it sends back have provided valuable data for astronomers.

An elliptical galaxy: a collection of stars shaped like a rugby ball or an American football.

REPAIRING THE HUBBLE SPACE TELESCOPE

I hope you brought a screwdriver.

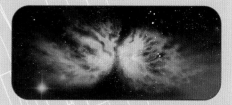

An irregular galaxy – one of the many astronomers can now study thanks to the HST. These galaxies contain large gas and dust clouds.

A spiral galaxy, one of the many space phenomena that HST and other probes have allowed scientists to observe.

The HST orbits the Earth every 97 minutes at a height of 600 kilometres. It is named after Edwin Hubble (1889–1953), the American astronomer.

Cutaway view of the Hubble Space Telescope

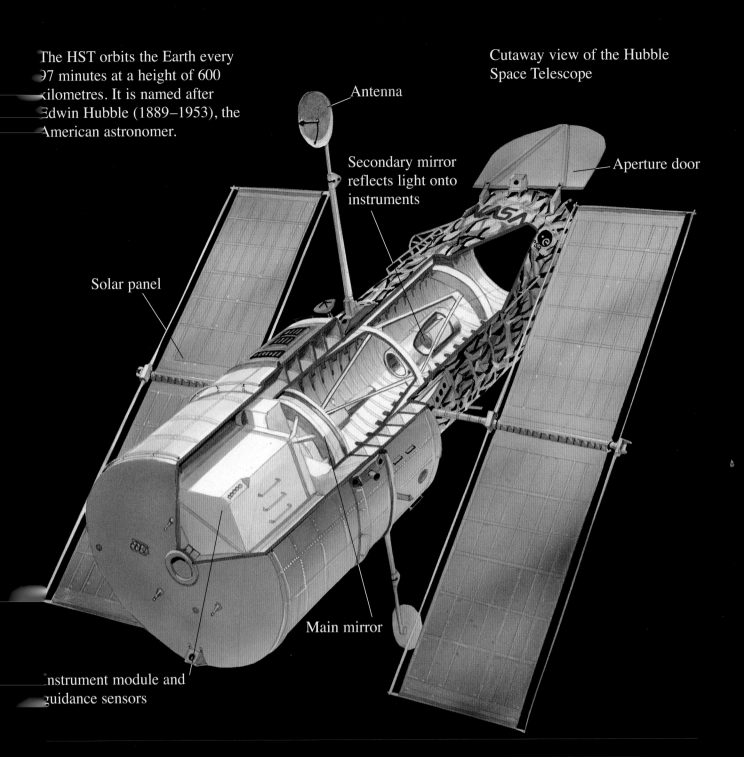

Antenna

Secondary mirror reflects light onto instruments

Aperture door

Solar panel

Main mirror

Instrument module and guidance sensors

The first images from HST were blurred, because the mirror system was faulty. Could it be repaired? After a year's training and five practice spacewalks, astronauts set off in the space shuttle *Endeavour*. The mission lasted 11 days and the repairs were successful.

After the loss of the space shuttle orbiter *Columbia* in February 2003, all flights to the HST were cancelled. This was a blow to astronomers because a flight had been planned for 2006 to install more sensitive cameras.

AMAZING FACT

Not all satellites are man-made: a satellite is any object that travels around another object, such as the Moon around the Earth.

REUSABLE CRAFT: DIFFERENT TYPES

Launch craft
White Knight

Now it is possible to design reusable spacecraft, the next challenge is to design a cheaper launch vehicle. The ideal would be a 'single stage to orbit' vehicle. This would not need booster rockets, which would make space launches much cheaper. Even so, the costs are enormous, and smaller countries wanting to take part in space research need to form joint ventures. The European Space Agency (ESA) is a good example of this.

The VentureStar or X-33 is a Fully Reusable Launch Vehicle (RLV) of the 'single stage to orbit' type.

SPACE TOURISTS

Wish you were here!

So far, space tourism is only for the super-rich. In April 2001 Dennis Tito's return ticket to the International Space Station cost $29 million!

The Energia booster rocket launched *Buran*, the Soviet Union's first space shuttle, in 1988. After a change of government the following year, the programme was halted.

Hermes shuttle
and Ariane rocket

Columbus space station
docked with Hermes

Hermes

The ESA developed the Hermes shuttle. It was quite small – 18
metres long with a 10-metre wingspan – and would have a crew of
six. However, it was cancelled because of the high cost.

The design of the Heavy-Lift Launch Vehicle (HLLV) is based on
the shuttle, with the same type of boosters and ET. The HLLV would
be used on unmanned missions to lift the heavy parts of a space
station into orbit.

Designs for an HLLV (top) and
a space plane (above).

SpaceShipOne, the first
privately financed manned
spacecraft, is designed to be
carried by the *White Knight*
launch craft shown opposite.

PROBES TO THE RED PLANET

Mariner 9

Mars gets its nickname 'the Red Planet' from its natural colour, which comes from the materials of which it is made. Probes are essential tools in learning about other planets. Unlike some planets, Mars is fairly close to Earth – 496 million kilometres. Since the American probe *Mariner 4* sent the first images of Mars back to Earth in July 1965, many other robotic missions have been sent to explore the planet.

In 1975 the US landed two Viking probes (below) on Mars. There were no signs of life, but the cameras sent back colour pictures of Mars's surface and atmosphere.

Ultra-high-frequency (UHF) antenna

Propellant tank

TV camera

Sample processor

Sampler heads and magnets

Descent engine

ALIENS ON MARS?

Take us to your leader!

Mars has been a source of myth and mystery for thousands of years – from the ancient Egyptians to modern film-makers. Stories about intelligent beings living on Mars began in the 19th century. From this it wasn't long before tales of 'little green men' from Mars invading Earth became popular.

MARS PATHFINDER

On 4 July 1997 the *Mars Pathfinder* landed on the planet. Its journey of 496 million kilometres had taken seven months. The probe was small and light, so the touch-down was risky – but *Pathfinder* landed successfully in the windswept valley of Ares Vallis. When it halted, the protective airbags retracted and solar panels opened out. When all the panels had opened, *Sojourner*, a tiny rover vehicle, rolled down a ramp and onto Mars's surface. *Sojourner* was equipped with instruments to take samples and tests. All of *Sojourner*'s operating instructions were sent live from NASA operators on Earth. Because the distance between Earth and the Moon is so great, the transmissions took 15 minutes to reach the rover.

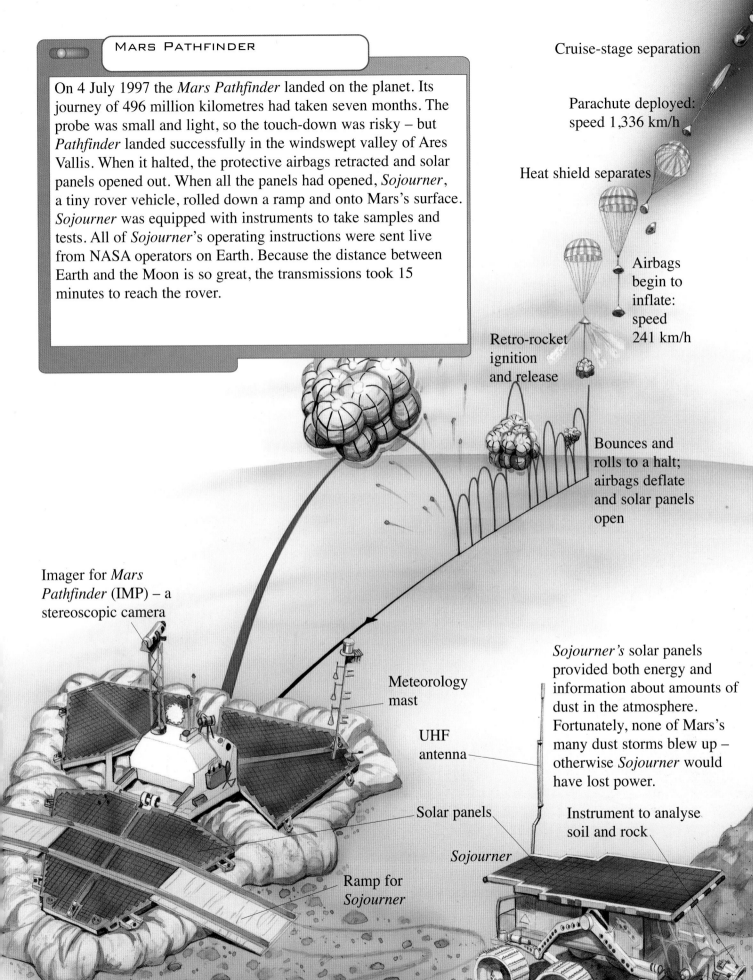

Cruise-stage separation

Parachute deployed: speed 1,336 km/h

Heat shield separates

Airbags begin to inflate: speed 241 km/h

Retro-rocket ignition and release

Bounces and rolls to a halt; airbags deflate and solar panels open

Imager for *Mars Pathfinder* (IMP) – a stereoscopic camera

Meteorology mast

UHF antenna

Sojourner's solar panels provided both energy and information about amounts of dust in the atmosphere. Fortunately, none of Mars's many dust storms blew up – otherwise *Sojourner* would have lost power.

Solar panels

Sojourner

Instrument to analyse soil and rock

Ramp for *Sojourner*

45

DISCOVERING MORE

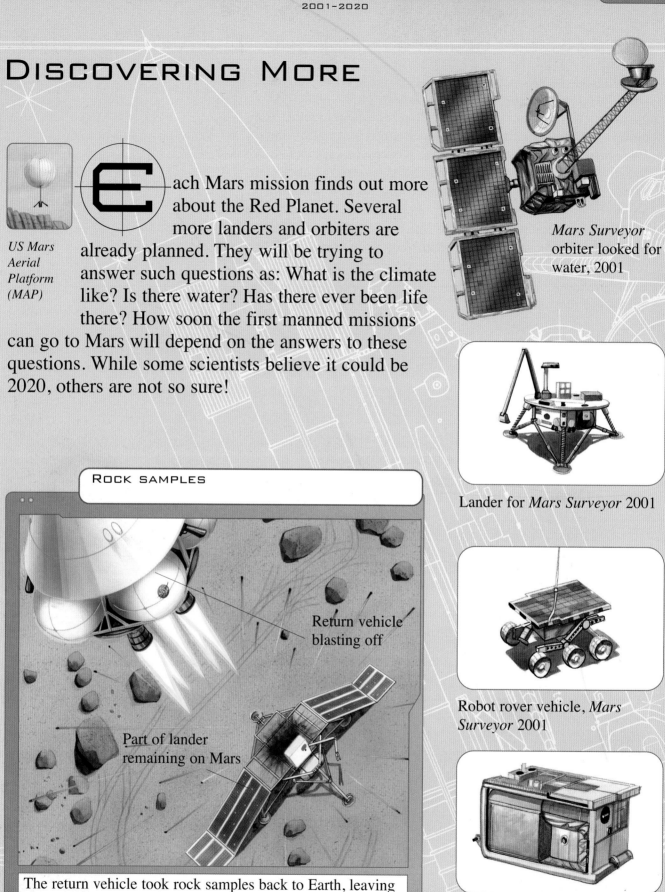

US Mars Aerial Platform (MAP)

Each Mars mission finds out more about the Red Planet. Several more landers and orbiters are already planned. They will be trying to answer such questions as: What is the climate like? Is there water? Has there ever been life there? How soon the first manned missions can go to Mars will depend on the answers to these questions. While some scientists believe it could be 2020, others are not so sure!

Mars Surveyor orbiter looked for water, 2001

Lander for *Mars Surveyor* 2001

Robot rover vehicle, *Mars Surveyor* 2001

Experimental chemical processor to make rocket fuel from gases in the atmosphere.

ROCK SAMPLES

Return vehicle blasting off

Part of lander remaining on Mars

The return vehicle took rock samples back to Earth, leaving the lander behind. This is designed to transmit information for another year.

Galileo spacecraft

On 18 October 1989 the space shuttle *Atlantis* launched the *Galileo* orbiter and probe on a mission to Jupiter. On 7 December 1995 the probe entered Jupiter's atmosphere, disintegrating after 58 minutes.

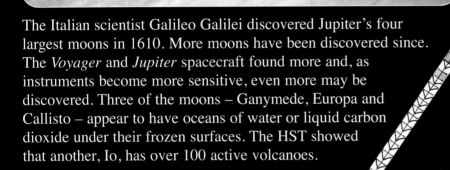

The Italian scientist Galileo Galilei discovered Jupiter's four largest moons in 1610. More moons have been discovered since. The *Voyager* and *Jupiter* spacecraft found more and, as instruments become more sensitive, even more may be discovered. Three of the moons – Ganymede, Europa and Callisto – appear to have oceans of water or liquid carbon dioxide under their frozen surfaces. The HST showed that another, Io, has over 100 active volcanoes.

In 1610 Galileo probably became the first person to see the rings of Saturn, saying they looked like 'cup handles' on each side of the planet. In 1659 Christiaan Huygens, the Dutch astronomer, realised they were rings which looked smooth and flat. It was centuries before astronomers were able to study them in more detail.

Saturn's winds blow at 500 metres per second.

LORD OF THE RINGS

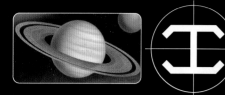

n October 1997 a US Titan 4B rocket blasted off carrying the *Cassini* orbiter and the ESA's (European Space Agency's) *Huygens* probe. Their destinations: Saturn's atmosphere and the surface of Titan, Saturn's largest moon. *Cassini* began orbiting Saturn on 30 June 2004, and *Huygens* landed on 14 January 2005.

Dense clouds surround Titan, but *Cassini*'s special imaging system could see through them to the planet's surface. As *Huygens* descended it sent back data about Titan's chemistry.

Saturn

Huygens probe enters Titan's atmosphere

Heat shield and probe separate

Titan

In space terms *Cassini* passed quite close to Saturn: 19,980 kilometres from the top of its dense clouds. The orbiter's cameras will take both close-up and wide-angle photographs of Saturn. Other instruments on board will 'map' minerals and chemicals, search for lightning and active volcanoes.

Saturn's rings actually consist of icy bits of rubble, from specks of dust to boulders. Each ring orbits the planet at a different speed.

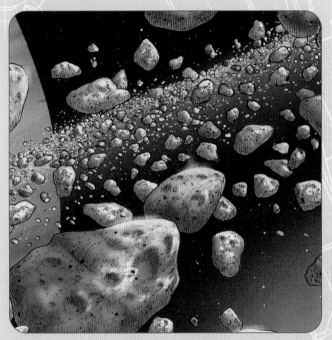

Huygens reached Titan's atmosphere, 1,200 kilometres above the planet's surface, travelling at 22,088 km/h. In three minutes this dropped to 1,450 km/h. The heat shield registered 11,980°C. At an altitude of 160 kilometres, the small pilot parachute pulled out the main, 8-metre-wide one. At 116 kilometres this was cut away and the 3-metre-wide stabiliser chute opened. Two and a half hours after beginning its descent, *Huygens* landed on Titan at 24 km/h.

Cassini

Huygens probe

Huygens landing sequence

Heat shield and first parachute separate from probe

Second parachute deployed, allowing probe to land

Huygens probe on Titan's surface

PRESENT AND FUTURE MISSIONS

Stardust probe, with the coma of a comet

s the technology gets better, it is possible to travel ever further in space – for those countries prepared to pay for it! In January 2004 NASA's *Stardust* probe flew through the dust and gas cloud around the comet Wild 2. Two years later, in January 2006, it parachuted to Earth with dust and other particles it had collected from the cloud. Scientists believe these will tell us about the origins of our own planet, Earth.

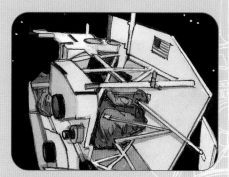

As planned, the space probe *Deep Impact* flew into the comet Tempel 1 on 4 July 2005. The craft had an ion engine, which is powered by the gas xenon charged with electricity.

CHINA JOINS THE SPACE AGE

A programme of national pride: October 2003 and China's first manned space flight is successful. On 11 October 2005 a two-man flight is also successful.

The HST 'sees' by detecting different types of light, from ultraviolet to infrared. The Herschel Space Observatory (above), due for launch by the ESA in 2008, will study distant space using far-infrared light.

The Chinese manned spacecraft Shenzhou ('Divine Ship') was built with Russian assistance and is like the Russian Soyuz. Four unmanned flights took place between 1999 and 2003. Then, in October 2003, Yang Liwei went into orbit in *Shenzhou 5*. Shenzhou (like Soyuz) has two modules: orbital and descent. After the two have separated, the orbital module, which has its own propulsion system, will remain in orbit as an unmanned vehicle for more research. Soyuz cannot do this.

In a speech on 14 January 2004 US President George W. Bush said NASA ought to rethink its space plans, ending the space-shuttle programme by 2010, when the ISS should be complete. Then there should be more manned flights to explore the solar system, with another Moon landing in 2020.

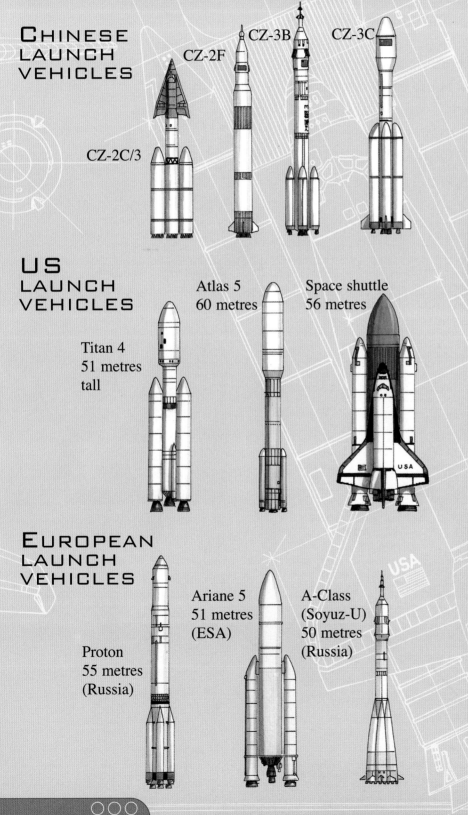

CHINESE LAUNCH VEHICLES

CZ-2C/3

CZ-2F

CZ-3B

CZ-3C

US LAUNCH VEHICLES

Titan 4
51 metres
tall

Atlas 5
60 metres

Space shuttle
56 metres

EUROPEAN LAUNCH VEHICLES

Proton
55 metres
(Russia)

Ariane 5
51 metres
(ESA)

A-Class
(Soyuz-U)
50 metres
(Russia)

Still at the earliest planning stages, how will this new Moon lander finally look?

THE INTERNATIONAL SPACE STATION

Because space exploration costs so much, most countries now co-operate in joint ventures. The largest is the International Space Station (ISS), which involves 16 countries. It was launched on 20 November 1998 to orbit 354 kilometres above the Earth. When complete it should weigh 453 tonnes and have a crew of seven. Unfortunately, rising costs and political pressure, especially in the US, have dogged the project. The ISS's future is uncertain.

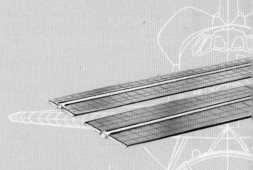

The solar panels measure 73.15 metres and provide all the electrical power the ISS needs.

WEIGHTLESSNESS IN SPACE

Zero gravity doesn't stop plants from growing.

Weightlessness in space affects humans, but it doesn't stop plants growing. Russian cosmonauts have successfully grown wheat in the *Mir* space station.

In 1984 President Ronald Regan suggested the US should have a manned space station. The cost forced President Clinton to make it an international effort in 1993. Construction of the ISS stopped after the destruction of the space shuttle *Columbia* during re-entry on 1 February 2003. Building restarted in 2005, and is currently scheduled for completion in 2010.

As designed, the ISS had a large living module for the crew. Each crew member had their own small cabin and slept in a wall-hung sleeping bag (page 53) – it's easy to sleep upright when you're weightless! When US space shuttle flights were stopped after the loss of *Columbia* in February 2003, all transport to and from the ISS was by the Russian *Soyuz* spacecraft.

The ISS allows scientists to test whether microgravity affects such things as growing crystals and making drugs.

SURVIVING IN SPACE

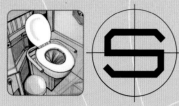

Sending astronauts to the planets is much more difficult than sending unmanned probes. For a start, the astronauts have to survive the journey. Going to Mars is a three-year round trip: it takes six to eight months to get there, followed by a stay of 18 months to two years until Earth and Mars align again, and then the journey back. The Russians, with more experience of space stations than the Americans, have contributed information gained from their cosmonauts' experiences on *Mir*.

A training capsule has been built at the Johnson Space Center. It has a closed-loop life-support system: nothing can be added to, or taken from, it.

Astronauts' food is dried or prepacked. Bean sprouts and quail eggs could be fresh food on long journeys.

The hearts and muscles of weightless astronauts do not have to work very hard, and soon weaken. Hard exercise every day prevents this.

NEW SPACESUITS FOR A MARS MISSION

A spacesuit weighs approximately 127 kg on the ground – without the astronaut in it. Of course, it weighs nothing in space. Putting it on, including the special underwear, takes 45 minutes.

The Mars Habitat Testbed Module on the ISS
will allow more research into the effects on
astronauts of the long voyage to the planet.

Mars Habitat
Testbed Module

One danger on the voyages to and from Mars is radiation from solar-flare storms. If such a storm occurs, the crew will shelter in a central airlock in the spacecraft's habitation module – but no-one knows if this protection will be enough.

Asleep in space:
an astronaut in his cabin.

Sheltering in
the airlock

Wall-hanging
sleeping bag

In their sleeping bags,
astronauts' heads and feet are
held in place with straps. If they
were not, their heads would flop
forward and their legs float
upwards.

PLANS TO REACH MARS

The problems with sending a manned mission to Mars are enormous. But, even so, in 1989, 20 years after the first Moon landing, US President George Bush asked NASA to do just that. They drew up a plan, based on the earlier Apollo missions, which would involve building an interplanetary spacecraft outside the Earth's atmosphere. However, it would take 30 years and cost $450 billion – if everything worked.

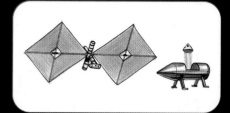

A Russian mission to Mars planned to use huge solar panels to power electric rocket motors, but they proved too slow.

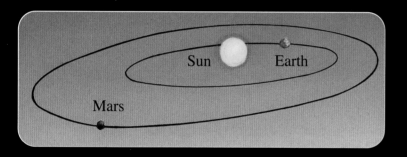

Sun   Earth

Mars

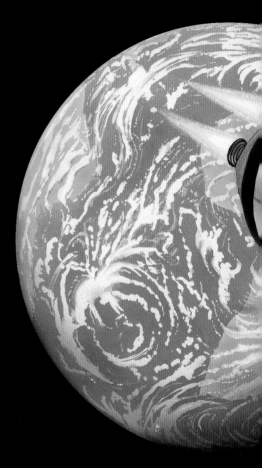

THREE YEARS IN SPACE

Are we nearly there yet?

AMAZING FACT

More than two-thirds of the fresh water on Earth is locked up in ice caps and glaciers. That is why the Martian ice caps are important (see page 59).

Because NASA's planned spacecraft (left) was too expensive, scientists looked for other options. There are two: the Mars Direct (below) and the Mars Semi-Direct (right).

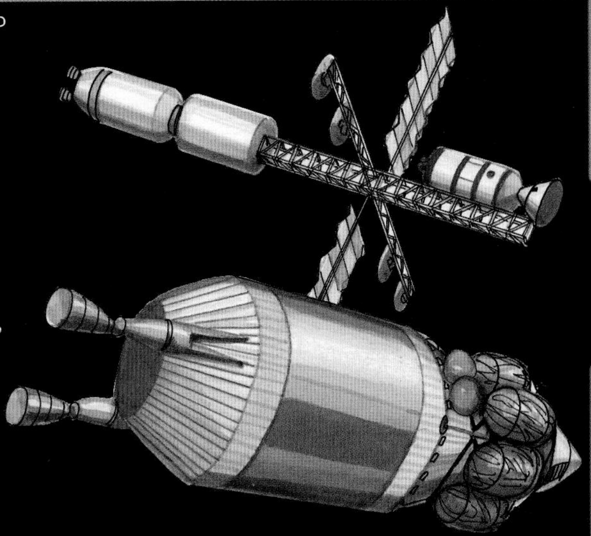

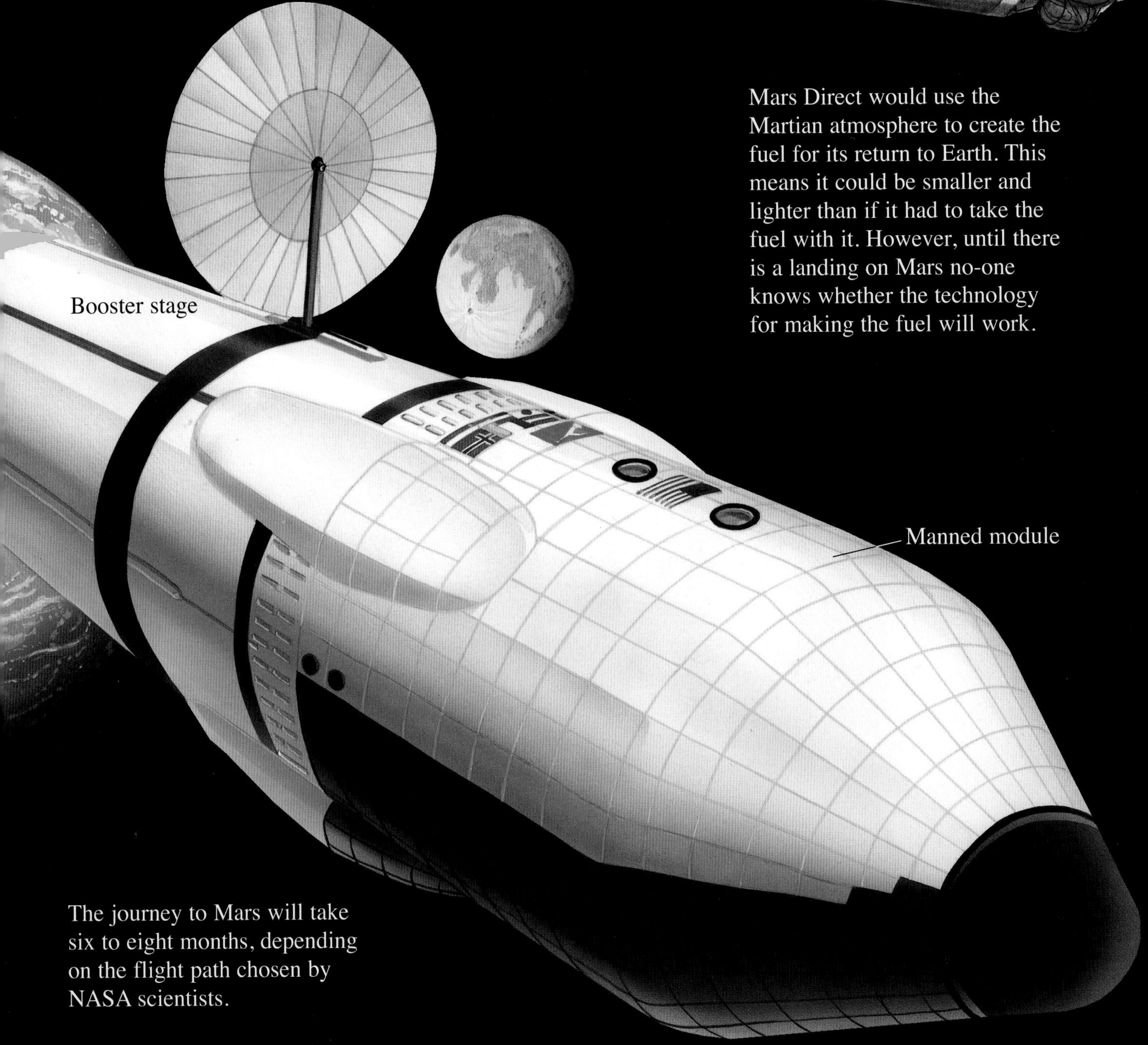

Mars Direct would use the Martian atmosphere to create the fuel for its return to Earth. This means it could be smaller and lighter than if it had to take the fuel with it. However, until there is a landing on Mars no-one knows whether the technology for making the fuel will work.

Booster stage

Manned module

The journey to Mars will take six to eight months, depending on the flight path chosen by NASA scientists.

FUTURE MARS LANDINGS

Approaching Mars, the booster stage is jettisoned

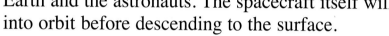hen the Mars Direct spacecraft reaches the Martian atmosphere it will jettison its booster stage because the fuel will have been used. The booster will probably be lost in deep space, but could become a relay station for communications between the command centre on Earth and the astronauts. The spacecraft itself will go into orbit before descending to the surface.

Mars is very dry and has frequent dust storms. One problem the crew may face is the damage this dust will do to their equipment. It could clog vital valves, scratch protective surfaces and even cause electrical faults.

A manned rover vehicle will help astronauts explore Mars. Rock and soil samples can be studied in the lander's laboratory.

Lander

Manned rover vehicle

SCOTT

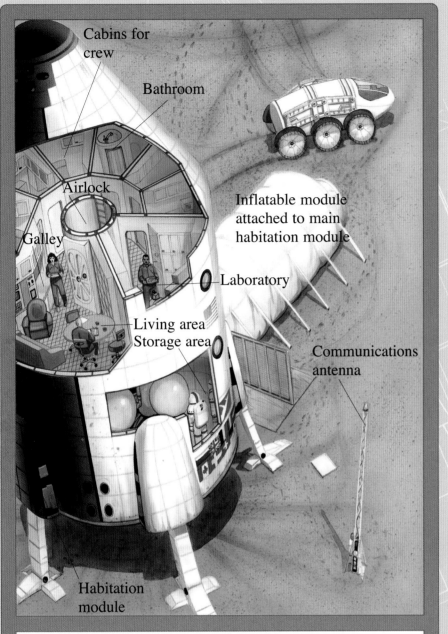

Cabins for
crew

Bathroom

Airlock

Galley

Inflatable module
attached to main
habitation module

Laboratory

Living area
Storage area

Communications
antenna

Habitation
module

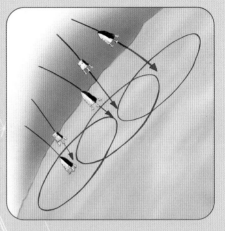

The planned timetable for Mars
Direct flights is:
Year 1: Robotic fuel plant lands.
Year 3: First crew arrives.
Year 5: Crew returns to Earth.
The spacecraft is powered by
fuel made by the fuel plant
landed in Year 1.
Year 5 or 6: Another fuel plant
is sent to make fuel for the next
manned mission. If all this is
successful, several bases could
be set up on Mars. However, the
astronauts face many problems,
including long exposure to
radiation and low gravity.

One crew member will be a geologist who will organise
collecting samples and set up sensors and seismometers to
measure 'Marsquakes'. Another will be a systems specialist to
deal with any problems with the lander or other equipment.
Again, radiation from solar flares could be a danger. Scientists
believe the Martian atmosphere will provide some protection,
and the lander's airlock provides more, but only a manned
landing will reveal the answer.

LIVING ON MARS

Could Mars ever look like this? NASA plans a manned mission, probably by 2020. And then? Mars is cooler than Earth, but also has seasons and 24-hour days – important for growing plants from Earth. Although dry, it has polar ice caps. So, if greenhouse gases were pumped into its atmosphere to warm it, melt the ice caps and create seas and rivers, perhaps humans could live there. But this would take time: 100 years for warming, 500 years to melt the ice!

COULD THIS BE MARS IN THE DISTANT FUTURE?

The first Mars base might look like this. Inflatable modules would give the astronauts more space. Plants for food could be grown in inflatable greenhouses.

'Terraforming' is the term for turning a planet like Mars into something more like Earth.

CHANGING THE MARTIAN CLIMATE

These two images show what might happen if the Martian atmosphere became warmer. As the polar ice caps slowly melted, the water would flow towards low-lying areas. There is a large area of lowland in the northern hemisphere and eventually this would fill to form an ocean. One reason warming Mars would take so long is that the surface temperature averages -60° C (Earth's average is 15° C). And that's another reason why it will be a very long time before humans can live there.

Humans cannot breathe the Martian air, so would need to wear oxygen tanks and masks wherever they went. In theory, terraforming might change the air, but there would be more urgent problems, such as getting plants to grow outdoors in the Martian ground.

THE DISTANT FUTURE

No-one knows how space exploration will develop. It could be stopped by a catastrophe on Earth. The dinosaurs, which had lived on Earth for millions of years longer than humans have, were wiped out, probably by a cosmic 'accident' – and this could happen again. But that doesn't prevent the scientists, or the science fiction writers, speculating. And, as the Earth becomes more polluted, overcrowded and altered by global warming, living in space is more appealing.

Some planners even see the planets, and communities in space (opposite), as the solution to overcrowded prisons on Earth. Depressingly, this is not a new idea. When Australia became a British colony in the 18th century, it was so far away from Britain that convicted criminals were sent there instead of prison. The environment was so hostile that if any escaped they had little chance of survival. This sounds rather like living in space or on another planet!

CITIES IN THE SOLAR SYSTEM

The planets vary so much, with different atmospheres, climates and so on, that humans would face different problems on each one.

This space colony was designed to solve the problem of overcrowding on Earth. It is intended to house thousands of people in an entirely self-contained and self-sufficient environment. The space station has an artificial landscape designed to mimic that of Earth, and artificial 'seasons'. Plants for food are grown in the pods that encircle the colony.

From the outside the space colony has no windows. Inside it looks quite different. Not only are there 'windows', but the view through them is constantly changing, just as it would if you were looking through real windows. The planners do this because the people inside would quickly become claustrophobic if they couldn't look out of the window.

Outer wall of space station

Artificial landscape inside space station

Mirror to reflect sunlight

Communications system

Pods for growing food plants

Glossary

altitude height, usually measured from sea level.

astronaut a specially trained person who travels in space.

atmosphere a layer of gases surrounding a planet.

booster a rocket engine which gives a burst (boost) of extra power at launch, and is then jettisoned.

capsule the part of a spacecraft in which the astronauts travel.

claustrophobic experiencing fear from being enclosed in a small space.

cosmonaut the Russian word for 'astronaut'.

docking the linking-up of two craft in space.

ESA European Space Agency – the organisation in charge of space research in Europe.

G a measure of the force of gravity.

geologist someone who studies the make-up of rocks.

gravity the force that attracts (pulls) something towards the centre of the Earth, or another body, such as the Sun or a planet.

HST Hubble Space Telescope.

ISS International Space Station.

jettison to throw away something that is no longer needed, such as an empty fuel tank or booster rocket.

lander the part of a spacecraft that lands on a planet or moon.

light-year the distance light travels in a year: 9,500 billion kilometres. It is a measurement of distance, *not* time.

liquid fuel a gas that has been cooled to become liquid, for use as rocket fuel.

LRV Lunar Roving Vehicle.

lunar to do with the Moon.

Mach a measure of speed; Mach 1 is the speed of sound.

Martian to do with Mars.

microgravity another name for weightlessness.

micrometeoroids minute particles of dust and rock littering space.

module a part of a spacecraft which can be detached and used separately from the other parts.

NASA National Aeronautics and Space Administration – the agency in charge of space research in the USA.

orbit the curved path made by one object as it travels around another.

orbiter a spacecraft, or a module of a spcecraft, which is intended to orbit a moon or planet.

payload the load carried by a vehicle, such as passengers on an aircraft or communications satellites on a spacecraft.

probe a robotic device controlled from Earth that explores and studies space.

propellant any kind of fuel burnt in a rocket engine to provide thrust.

rover a wheeled vehicle for exploring a planet's surface.

solar flare a burst of electrically charged particles from the Sun.

Soviet Union or **USSR** (Union of Soviet Socialist Republics) a country consisting of Russia and several other states, united under a single government until 1991.

terraforming altering a planet to make it more like Earth, so humans may be able to live there.

thrust the pushing force made by a rocket engine.

weightlessness the condition experienced by astronauts in orbiting spacecraft: they float as if they really had no weight.

zero gravity the conditon of weightlessness existing beyond the pull of gravity.

INDEX

MISSION BADGES

1

2

3

4

5

6

7

8